Sl

Down

By

Robert Campbell

Thanks

Firstly thanks to my children for wanting me to tell them stories. I have an ever ready and willing to comment focus group of three! If they're happy, then I'm happy.

Next, thanks to my wife Esther for all her hard work proof reading, honing and removing my excess use of commas!

Thanks to Angelina King for her suggestions and observations. She is an excellent author and you can check out her work at www.angelineking.com

I'm also grateful to Julie Young and Siabhra Henry for pre-reading the book and offering comments.

Contents

Saturday December 21st, Sunrise

Their school jumpers were neatly folded away for Christmas.

It was now just four days to the big day! It was also the shortest day of the year. The four friends gathered to watch the sunrise as they did every year. There they sat together: Susan the sheep, Ralph the buzzard, Finbar the mouse and Betty the collie dog. They were the best of friends, and better still they were all in the same class at school.

It was a beautiful morning. The heavy frost made everything look so Christmassy. Most creatures loved it, except for spiders. They hated the big heavy cold white blanket of frost that weighed down their webs to breaking point. The spiders often remarked, *"They wouldn't like it if their houses were all covered in frost!"* But everyone else thought it looked pretty, and was oh so much like Christmas! Sitting in front of the whin and hawthorn hedge the four friends peacefully waited.

Far away at the North Pole, things were not so peaceful. In fact things were really very tense and very fraught. It was not nice at all. You see the elves were behind in their work. So far behind, no one could believe just how far behind they were!

Since early summer, every time Santa asked how the work was going, they told him, *"It's going great!"* They were telling Santa the truth because they really believed it was going well.

However, had they told Santa the detail instead of just saying, "*It's going great,*" he would have realised it wasn't going great at all and would have been able to help.

You see, the new power unit for the sled had taken ages to arrive from Homey Airport. Then it took much longer than expected to fit. On top of that, because it was more powerful than they had anticipated, the whole break and suspension system had to be completely stripped down, redesigned and rebuilt. This meant the sled needed to be totally refitted because they weren't sure it could cope with the force produced by the powerful new engine!

At the same time as the four friends were watching the sunrise, two elves were pushing the revamped sled into the test tunnel. One elf had a round friendly face, while the other looked rather cheeky.

The sled came out of the test tunnel unscathed. Now they could finally take it out for a 'Down and Round'. That's when you fly down from the North Pole to the South Pole and come back up round the other side. If this worked they would take it for a Dress Rehearsal tomorrow with the reindeer and pretend presents.

The two elves got into the sled and gave the engine a massive rev. Instead of revving loudly, the engine pleasantly hummed. *"That doesn't sound exciting,"* the cheeky elf remarked. *"But it was going pretty well in the test tunnel,"* the elf with the round friendly face replied.

The sled was sitting on the ice runway, ready for the Down and Round. The cheeky elf who was driving called, *"I'll do the countdown"*. He shouted really quickly, *"10-9-8-7-6-5-4-3-2"* but before he got '1' out, the sled had fired down the ice runway and shot into the sky!

They had forgotten to attach the safety beacon - a really bad oversight - but they were back at the North Pole so quickly no one realised they were gone. They had flown so high in the sky they only just remained within the atmosphere, and they were only spotted once. Well, their reflection in the rising sun was spotted as they zipped past Culmore.

Back at base the checks were all completed and the sled pronounced ready for the Dress Rehearsal. The elf with the cheeky face stuck the safety beacon to the back of the sled with masking tape and then ticked the box on the check list that read, "*safety beacon securely attached*".

Where the four friends sat was flat. Nearby, the land started to slope downwards, sometimes quickly, sometimes slowly but always downward. It didn't stop until it reached the stream at the bottom of the field. Here the water bubbled over stones as it meandered towards Lough Foyle. Behind the stream was a hedge and behind the hedge were some big trees. The lough was wide and long. At one end it fed into the Atlantic Ocean while at the other end the River Foyle fed into Lough Foyle. Across the lough were the hills, now extremely black against the cloudless orange sky.

Ralph the buzzard was running through his calculations but this was brought to an abrupt end when Susan the sheep exclaimed, "*I think it's about to happen!*" "*You always say that,*" squeaked Finbar the mouse. Ralph replied, "*When has it not happened?*" Finbar was desperate to say, "*It always happens*" just to prove he knew, but he realised the right answer was the wrong one to give, so he didn't speak (which was unusual for him!).

A little robin landed in the hedge, dismissively looked at them, ate a red holly berry, sang a cheery song and flew away. The sky that had been orange was now an incredible golden colour. Then the rising sun appeared. It was an extra bright orangey ball, nearly impossible to look at. Now boys and girls, it is important to realise that for human children it is dangerous to stare at the sun! But as the animal children watched the sunrise, they noticed a tiny flash of light shooting through the sky.

Though they didn't realise at the time, they had just caught the reflection of Santa's sled doing its Down and Round!

Sunday December 22nd, Tea Time

Betty the collie dog was worried by what she'd seen this afternoon. Today was Sunday the 22nd of December, just two days before Christmas Eve and something had gone wrong, very wrong! Although she didn't know it, the Dress Rehearsal of Santa's sled had happened today, and what the four friends had seen between them earlier that afternoon was the bitter end of that Dress Rehearsal! Betty confided her concerns to Finbar but he thought she always worried too much so didn't pay much heed.

For some reason the elves had used the Foyle for their route. They whizzed down the river towards the lough, but never mind getting back to the North

Pole, they'd only just managed to get beyond Culmore Point before they crashed!

To go back a bit and explain what had happened. The elves had been travelling along the lough at breakneck speed. When they reached the Craigavon Bridge (the blue double-decker one), they hurtled between the decks (the rule book said they weren't to do that).

Next was the Peace Bridge (the swirly-whirly foot bridge with the sharp pointy bits, the one in all the pictures). Instead of going high over it as they were meant to, they went high, really high, way up high into the sky. Then, at the top of going up really high, they came down really, really, REALLY quickly, so quickly they could hardly see! They went under the Peace Bridge (the rule book said they weren't to do that either, but they seemed to be ignoring the rule book a lot today).

While flying under the Peace Bridge they clipped the water and bounced like a skimming stone past the shops, past the opulent council buildings, past the fishing boat someone seemed to have abandoned and on towards the Foyle Bridge (the high one with the big hump). There was plenty of room to go below the bridge and plenty of time to get over it, but instead, the elf with the cheeky face aimed straight at it!

I need to tell you a little story of Christmas past. Last Christmas Eve while cleaning up the main dispatch room, the elf with the cheeky face had found a pull-string Evel Knievel toy from the 1970s (you'll need to ask your parents...oh dear...maybe grandparents about this)! Since then he'd been playing with it and was pretending the Foyle Bridge was his 'Grand Canyon'.

He looped the sled round the Foyle Bridge six times before firing on up the lough towards Lisahally Docks. He knew that large and dangerous electric lines crossed at Culmore Point, and that elves and humans and animals must be exceptionally careful with electric cables! So he made the sled dive down to a safer height. They went under the lines, but clipped the top of Culmore Fort!

At this point they made their biggest mistake. Instead of continuing on to the Atlantic Ocean and to the North Pole, they banked hard to the left. The cheeky elf had decided they were going for another loop around the bridges.

But disaster struck!

They were going too fast;

They didn't make enough height; and clipped the top of Culmore fort;

They sheared the top of a tree on Iskaheen hill;

They went into a tailspin...

and crashed into the soft boggy ground!

The only positive was that they didn't actually bang into a tree, although this didn't stop the sled crumpling as it hit and partly sunk into the soft, water-logged ground!

Miraculously no one was hurt. In the confusion three reindeer ran off. The elves, whose heads were still spinning from whizzing round the bridges, from the tail spin and from the crash, flopped down on the sodden moss, their bottoms getting wetter by the second.

They looked at each other, dazed, the realisation of what they had done just starting to dawn!

Now, it is important to realise something. Human children and animal children are different. Human children's eyes are not adjusted to see what had just happened, although admittedly a few children walking over the Peace Bridge had noticed strange, bouncy, ripply things on the water.

However, when the four animal children pieced everything together, they had seen most of what had just happened! Their head teacher, the Wise Old Owl had also somehow heard about the crash (you must remember that owls are always wise and that head teachers always hear).

Though the school was closed for the Christmas holidays, the four friends were summoned back immediately! They put on their school jumpers and quickly made their way to the building. It was quiet when they arrived. No children playing in the playground, no children talking in class (though they weren't meant to talk during lessons), no children singing (which sometimes was a good thing), no children learning and thinking (it is important to take a break from the hard work).

Everyone else was at home full of excitement, for it was now just two days until Christmas Eve. Santa letters had been sent and hopes were high, in some cases far too high!

Having pressed the buzzer and been admitted, the four hung up their coats in the cloakroom and Ralph the buzzard went to the toilet. Then everyone assembled in the computer room. Here they were met with hot chocolate and a healthy snack, though Finbar the mouse wondered at the prudence of a half measure. If allowed hot chocolate, why not chocolate biscuits too? Was there really any need for this 'healthy snack carry-on' so near Christmas?

"*Hello children,*" said the head teacher. "*Hello Mrs Wise Owl,*" the four friends replied.

"*I'm sure you're surprised to be back at school so soon,*" she said.

"*Yea, great, I really wanted to be back at school during the Christmas holidays,*" Finbar said under his breath.

"*Sorry Finbar, I didn't catch that,*" the Wise Old Owl responded, knowing exactly what he had said.

"*Oh, nothing Miss,*" he mumbled.

She smiled and went on, "*We are back at school because something has happened. Something bad has happened. None of you did it, but I need your help to fix it or lots of children will be extraordinarily sad this year!*"

Monday December 23rd, Morning

Ever since the crash the elves had been working feverishly. They gathered branches, leaves and grass to cover the sled -

to hide it;

to stop it being found;

to stop it being photographed;

to stop it being filmed;

to stop pictures being posted on the World Wide Web.

For should a Santa-Hunt start, people and news crews would descend on the forest from all over the world. They could just hear the news headlines:

"Has Santa's sled been found?"

"Will there be presents this year?"

That would be bad enough, but what would Santa say? You never really think of Santa being cross, but the elves knew that Santa can be cross. This doesn't happen very often, but when he is cross, he is really cross, especially when his sled has been needlessly crashed two days before Christmas!

The cheeky elf threw a final handful of leaves unto the heap. It was invisible at last...well it was actually hidden, not invisible, but you know what I mean!

This was a big year, one of those really big and busy years. The letters had been arriving thick and fast for months. The Big Man's phone started pinging with e-mails in May and hadn't stopped since! That meant he needed his biggest sled this year to be in tip top, super duper working order to cope with the pressure. But its old engine hadn't been working well. In fact it had been running pretty poorly. Sometimes it went poop. . .poop. . .poop and then cut out!

It had been sent to the Elvish Engineering Department, the EED for repair in early summer. Since then they'd been working at it, and finally in the mouth of Christmas, it was not only fixed, but running better than ever before!

The reindeer, full crew (except the Big Guy) and the equivalent weight of toys were all on board for the Dress Rehearsal and everything had gone extraordinarily well until they crashed.

Now in a forest, looking down on Lough Foyle, having just hidden Santa's smashed sled, they counted the reindeer: one, two, three, four, five, six...

They counted again: one, two, three, four, five, six...

They called the roll and realised that Dancer, Prancer and Rudolph were missing. A bad day had just become even worse!

At school the four children told the Wise Old Owl exactly what they each had witnessed. The mouse, Finbar was on the Craigavon Bridge when he saw the sled hurtle down the Foyle and in between the decks of the bridge.

At that time Betty the collie dog was out for a walk over the Peace Bridge and through St. Columb's Park. Just as she raised her head from following a 'sniff trail' she caught sight of the sled bursting out from between the decks of the Craigavon Bridge, shooting up into the sky, diving down below the Peace Bridge, skimming along the water and round the bend of the lough.

Ralph the buzzard was high in the sky above Culmore. He watched the sled loop round the Foyle Bridge, then fire towards Culmore Point and clip the fort. At this point he went down to check the fort for damage.

Finally, Susan the sheep who had been peacefully grazing in a field saw the sled sail through the sky like a meteorite, trying to gain height to get over Iskaheen hill, and watched it shear the top of the tree before going into a tailspin and disappearing into the wood.

The Wise Old Owl, realising just how bad the situation was, smiled grimly and said, *"Thank you children".*

The three reindeer had scattered in different directions. Rudolph headed back to the city. Whilst hurtling up the Foyle near the Guildhall, he had caught a glance of Derry's Walls and there saw someone who appeared to be Santa Claus. He was a rather unconvincing Santa Claus, but, did you know that Santa Claus, when he wants to go out unseen, disguises himself as an unconvincing Santa Claus?! And guess what...it works! You've probably seen him lots of times but just thought he was someone making a poor show of pretending to be the real Santa. In these dire circumstances Rudolph hoped it was the real Santa dressed up as an unconvincing Santa. So with his nose unhelpfully glowing in the gloomy morning light of December 23rd, he decided to try to get help!

Dancer was a friendly reindeer. Shortly after fleeing the crash for fear of the sled exploding (it was fuelled by some kind of secretive fuel cell the elves had bought in from Nevada, something they had done without Santa's full knowledge), Dancer had made friends with a herd of cows.

These were unusual cows for the area. They weren't black and white Friesian milking cows like all the rest. No, these were gingery, sandy, fawn coloured highland cattle with shaggy coats and massive horns. They were a similar kind of colour to Dancer. Well...Dancer was a grey and white colour, but it was better than nothing, and being with the herd did make her harder to spot!

The highland cattle didn't believe Dancer's story about flying sleds and crashes. They hadn't seen the sled shoot through the sky as at that moment they were busily devouring a feeder of fresh hay the farmer had just left for them!

Prancer, always practical had decided to try to find a way home to the North Pole. He headed to Greencastle and sneaked unto the ferry to Magilligan. This wasn't an easy thing for a reindeer to do!

From there he made his way to Portrush. His goal was to board the polar expeditionary vessel, the Sir David Attenborough (or as it should be called, 'Boaty McBoatface'). Prancer had noticed it when flying along the north Antrim coast earlier. It had been visiting and was leaving that afternoon.

Boaty McBoatface, okay, the Sir David Attenborough was heading to the

Antarctic for Christmas, and if Prancer was really quick he might just catch a lift home.

Monday December 23rd, Mid-Morning

The Wise Old Owl sent Ralph the buzzard on a special mission to look for the sled from above. Ralph went unto the roof of the school (something human children must never do) and all the way up to the little bell tower where there is no bell anymore. He spread his wings, flapped them to gain height, circled a few times, and then gracefully and with great speed set off to look for Santa's crashed sled!

Ralph was so high in the sky that from the ground he looked like a little dot. He had decided to follow the lough and not the main road. He flew down over the houses behind the school. Then at the water he turned left, over Victoria Community Hall, over the water works, over the farmland and over the Country Park full of walkers out enjoying the beauty of nature. On and on he went. He passed Muff and then cut inland towards the forest on Iskaheen hill.

Had he followed the main road, Ralph would have noticed a sad looking reindeer with a slightly illuminated nose walking along the footpath. But as he hadn't, he didn't see the red-nosed reindeer and his slightly shining nose!

At the school the Wise Old Owl had wisely closed the curtains. Had they been open she too might have observed the real Rudolph trotting past. As it was, no one noticed him!

Now above the forest, Ralph the buzzard circled and circled. His sharp eyes peered down, searching every inch of the canopy; looking and looking and looking. Then he spotted something. He hadn't found the sled because it was so well hidden, but he did see broken branches high in the tree line.

He circled over this spot, and looking even more closely he caught sight of the mound of branches, leaves and twigs that hid the sled. He continued to gaze at this unusual pile and eventually glimpsed just the slightest movement. It lasted no more than a split second but it was enough! He'd just caught a glimpse of an elf. Their hiding place was found. He circled round and headed back to school as swiftly as his wings would take him.

Rudolph reached the Walls, but now was tied to one of the cannons! Until that point his journey had been without incident. People in passing cars (any who actually noticed him) just thought the reindeer was one of the more elaborate Christmas decorations - people do get a little carried away nowadays!

Rudolph had quickly found out that the Santa Claus on the Walls was not a real Santa Claus, nor was he a nice one. At first he had been kind, but once he gained Rudolph's trust, he tied him up and was now charging people £5 to have their picture taken with him. This enterprise was proving popular and a long queue had formed. A very long queue in fact. After 15 minutes it stretched a quarter of the way round the Walls. After 30 minutes it was half way round, and then on the hour the tip of the tail met the head of the line.

The shock of the crash was wearing off Rudolph and the multitude of carrots he was being fed meant his strength was returning quickly. This strength had reached his nose which was now glowing brightly. Even better, the tingle of flight had returned to his body!

As the other three children and the Wise Old Owl waited for Ralph to return, somehow the Wise Old Owl was informed of the happenings on Derry's Walls (you must remember that head teachers always know). She did not know the whole story but had gleaned enough to decide it would be wise to send Betty the collie dog and Finbar the mouse to investigate.

Should they find Rudolph and it really was Rudolph, Finbar was to bite through the rope just like his hero Reepicheep, and release Rudolph from his tether. That was the plan, the best they could come up with given the circumstances.

The two left school quickly and made their way down the Culmore Road. Before the roundabout they crossed at the lights (you must remember that it is always important for human children or talking animals to be particularly careful crossing busy roads).

Soon they were on the Walls where they followed the line of people and eventually found Rudolph whose nose was now glowing extraordinarily brightly. The false Santa was sitting nearby taking a break and a big black cat was lolling on the cannon right where the rope was tied!

Betty carried Finbar as close as she could. He jumped off her back, silently landed on the ground and scampered towards Rudolph. Betty was a strong brave dog. On more than one occasion she had chased other dogs away from the flock. These were normally town dogs that silly people had allowed to roam about the countryside without a lead. She wasn't scared of the cat, but whose cat was it? Did it belong to the false Santa Claus who had captured the real Rudolph, or was it a town cat hanging about for tit bits? Betty just didn't know.

Finbar had reached the cannon without drawing the attention of the cat...that was until now! It stood up, lowering its body ready to pounce. As Betty ran forward barking, the cat looked at her, appearing to smirk. Then it realised there was no lead, or human to protect it from this furious barking dog! Off it fled with a hiss and a screech, hair on end! Now the cat was gone, Finbar scurried up the cannon and started to bite his way through the rope. With each gnaw of his sharp little teeth the rope was soon severed and the tether fell limp on the ground. Rudolph was free!

Monday December 23rd, Lunch Time

Ralph flew straight (or as humans would say, 'as the crow flies') from the forest to the school (did you know that crows' feathered kinsfolk find this statement a little annoying? Whether humans realise it or not, other birds and not just crows can fly in straight lines!).

Long before he landed, his keen senses told him lunch had arrived. It was tasty hot food from one of the local shops. He subdued his pangs of hunger and went first to the Wise Old Owl's office. Perched on the arm of a chair, Ralph told her everything he had seen. The Wise Old Owl listened intently, thanked him for his clear report and sent him off for lunch with an extra scoop of ice cream!

The situation was awful, not just for these four or the children of the city, but children everywhere! Instead of eating her lunch, (some tasty sandwiches), the Wise Old Owl moved to the peace of the bottom playground to think.

Here's what she was thinking. It was obvious that the elves had hidden the sled. They didn't want footage taken, social media posts going viral, Santa Claus Hunts and all that sort of thing. But why had they hidden it rather than flying away? The only possible answer was that it had been too badly damaged to move.

She would have to make contact with the elves and this wouldn't be easy.

Dear knows what 'Santa Secrecy' potions and devices they were armed with to keep prying eyes away! The Wise Old Owl returned to her office, closed the door and began to make a few discreet phone calls. No matter the danger they may face, they still needed to help. After all this was Christmas Eve's Eve!

Rudolph, reindeer of shining red nose fame, Betty the collie dog and Finbar the mouse attempted to quietly slip away from the Walls. They vainly tried to discreetly nudge through the crowd, hoping that a mouse, collie dog and reindeer (one with a bright shining nose) would melt into the throng.

But the false Santa Claus spotted them. When I say, '*spotted them*', he spotted that Rudolph was gone and in a blind panic started roaring at the top of his voice, *"Where's my reindeer?! Where's my reindeer?!"* In mid-sneak to freedom they were discovered! The false Santa gave chase.

In that one morning the false Santa had earned more money than in all the last ten years together as a false Santa. The queue was now on its second lap around the Walls. There was a lot of money to be gained or lost. Never mind this afternoon, imagine the crowds Rudolph's nose glowing in the dark would attract tonight, and tomorrow, Christmas Eve! *"Come back!"* his voice boomed over the hubbub of the people on the Walls.

Hearing the voice and knowing they had been spotted, Rudoph and Betty sped away. Finbar, though scampering as quickly as he could, was rapidly being left behind. On realising this Betty slowed down and shouted to him, "*Jump on my back and hold tight!*" He did this without argument (most unusual for him). But soon, Betty and Finbar (who was clinging on for dear life as he bounced about on Betty's back) were being left behind by Rudolph! Worse still, the false Santa Claus was quickly catching up. Though his face was a bright red puce colour and he was panting for breath, the prospect of such a huge financial loss supplied him with a speed and stamina you would hardly credit, especially given the size of his girth - a part of the false Santa that was definitely real!

Rudolph had realised their plight straightaway. After all he is one of Santa's Reindeer, a group of highly intelligent animals who also can fly - a very unusual gift to possess unless you happen to be a bird. Rudolph slowed and shouted, *"Jump...jump unto my back and hold tight!"*.

So many people had come to see the reindeer with the now brightly glowing nose. Even the sceptics were willing to pay their £5 to get a closer look so they could try to work out how the nose was lit. Rudolph's path was blocked. People stood with their arms out, hoping to stop the reindeer and return it to who they believed was its rightful owner. Rudolph roared to Betty and Finbar, *"Hold Tight!"*

With that he leapt into the air - up and up and up into the air, high above the Millennium Forum, above the shops, the lough, the Waterside Theatre - and then the brightly glowing nose disappeared into the clouds! While the people watched in amazement the false Santa

Claus whispered awfully bad words under his breath.

Betty and Finbar clung unto Rudolph for dear life.

The people didn't believe the false Santa was the real Santa, but they had been impressed by the real Rudolph who they had assumed was a false Rudolph. It's all a bit confusing but I'm sure you know what I mean. The people had assumed that the brightly glowing nose was part of the act, and the flying reindeer was an even more spectacular part of the same show!

As Rudolph, Betty and Finbar disappeared into the sky the crowd responded with applause, cheering and a few whistles. They could not understand how this had happened but they congratulated the false Santa Claus for such an excellent performance! He quickly took off his hat, lifted a collection from the people and headed off in a more buoyant mood.

In less than one minute Rudolph and his passengers were back at school (you must remember that flying reindeer can travel the world in one evening). Rudolph, Betty and Finbar were hastily ushered into the hall, the one just through the main doors on the left. The Wise Old Owl knew Rudolph needed to be safely hidden and the school was a good place to hide.

Already the North West reporter for the local news station had arrived at the Walls, thankfully just after Rudolph had left. Eventually the reporter tracked down the bedraggled looking false Santa Claus. The interview was dreadful. He constantly repeated three well rehearsed phrases: "*It's the magic of Christmas*"; "*I just do it to put a smile on the children's faces*"; but mostly he kept saying, "*I make no money from it*". These had been learned for the benefit of the taxman rather than the press. The interview was so pathetic that the producer rolled her eyes. "*What a lot of nonsense,*" she thought and thankfully never used it!

After giving Rudolph a short break, the Wise Old Owl came into the school hall and they had a long private chat. From this she learned the sled had been smashed and could not fly. Rudolph was unsure as to the extent of the damage though as he had left the scene so quickly to seek help.

Monday December 23rd, Late Afternoon, Nearly Dark

It was getting dark, even though it was only about half past three. This far north the winter nights are long! It was the last chance to go outside, to run about or play games...or rescue Santa's sled!

Susan the sheep was scared, but she was being brave and she would follow through even though she had never done anything like this before! The Wise Old Owl had placed a chair beside the table and a step below the chair. Susan had cleared the step and was now on the chair. No one spoke as she got her front hoofs unto the table, but they all watched expectantly. As her weight moved from the chair to the table, the table wobbled. With this she snapped (something that was unusual for her), "*Are you holding that table still*?" Who she snapped *at* was rather unclear as no one was near the table. "*You're nearly there*," the Wise Old Owl encouraged. With a final careful flick of her rear legs she was on the table.

She had faced her fears; done what seemed impossible; she had reached where she needed to be! Susan took a deep breath and told herself, "*I can do this*". With one more determined movement she was on Rudolph's back.

The reindeer held still and then started off so smoothly Susan didn't realise he was moving at all. "*Hold on tight, Susan,*" Rudolph reminded her as he walked to the upper playground. Once they had reached the far edge, he turned and began to run at great speed. Susan started to speak but all that came out was a tiny little bleat. She tried again, but as she did they leapt into the air and all at once they were flying!

The plan was for Rudolph to leave Susan near the crash site. Rudolph couldn't return to the elves and other reindeer just yet as he was still needed by the Wise Old Owl. Instead, Susan would have to make contact with the elves herself.

They zipped through the twilight sky extraordinarily quickly. Susan, who had never left the comfort of ground before, kept her eyes shut for most of the journey. *"We're going down now,"* Rudolph told her. *"We'll land on the lane. You go behind the hedge and I'll leave straight away."*

The first Susan realised they were no longer flying was when she heard the sound of hooves running along the ground. The landing was so smooth that she hadn't felt even the slightest little bump. Rudolph hunkered down and Susan jumped off. No sooner was she on the ground than Rudolph was back in the air and heading to the school.

The sun had just set, the sky illumined with a wonderful dark blue glow. Head teacher Wise Owl made several more phone calls but the school friends and Rudolph had no idea to whom. She left word that she must go out and flew down towards the lough, over the water and away.

The plan was simple. Susan was to hide until it was completely dark. Then she would come out and go straight to the crash site. A lone sheep would raise the least suspicion. But as she was about to exit her hiding place at the far side of the lane (a lane that no one drove along in the dark), lights appeared!

The lights belonged to an old white van. Susan could not believe it. She crouched down, backing herself further into the hedge. The van stopped right beside her and though she did not know him, the false Santa Claus got out. He walked to the back of the van only a few feet from Susan, opened the doors and awkwardly climbed inside. She was terrified. Should she make a run for it or stay put? Susan was worried that if she ran she might not find the hole in the hedge in the darkness, the hole she needed to go through. So she didn't move.

A few moments later the false Santa Claus emerged from the van with an old TV. He threw it unto the ground, *crash!*

Once he did this he went and got another one and threw it on the ground, *smash!*

He did this four times in all!

People were making room for the new TVs that they hoped would arrive the morning after next.

Then he appeared with a few old mattresses, some furniture and finally he pushed a heap of assorted junk from the van unto the ground.

Susan's mood had changed from fear to anger! It was all she could do to stop herself from running out and shouting at this horrid man to jolly well pick up all his rubbish and take it back home with him; to yell at him, "*When you go into the countryside leave no trace!*"

The false Santa had been paid to collect this junk and take it to the dump, but instead of taking it there where he had to queue, he brought it into the countryside and threw it out. Though he didn't know it, this was the first time he had been caught!

He got into the van and drove away with his lights switched off to avoid any scrutiny (a dangerous action, not to be copied). Little did he know that Susan had already memorised his registration number to share with the local police and council!

When she was sure the van had left, Susan, wide eyed and still very annoyed, moved through the small opening in the hedge, past the newly deposited rubbish, over the lane and into the trees.

This part of the forest was old. The trees were gnarly and bare of leaves. The ground was undulating and covered in a carpet of soft bright green moss. She counted her steps whilst following the landmarks. There it was - the mound of sticks and leaves - Santa's sled!

Two little sets of irritated elfish eyes peered out from the trees. Further back, six sets of hopeful eyes looked upon this lone sheep. She moved closer to the sled, not seeing anyone because they were all so well hidden.

Then it happened! One of the elves blew a handful of magic dust at her - sparkly purple and red glowing stuff. Susan didn't see it until it was too late (you must understand that human children never see the powder at all; the powder that places you in a deep sleep and causes pleasant Christmas dreams). Just before succumbing to the magic she managed to bleat, *"Rudolph brought me. I'm here to helllllllll -"*.

The next thing Susan knew, it was morning.

Christmas Eve, Very Early Morning

The magic powder had worn off. Susan was sleeping naturally and the wonderful dreams had ended. When she woke up very early the next morning, the first thing she saw were two elves and six reindeer peering down on her.

Elves have a sense of when people are about to wake up. That's another reason why you never see them on Christmas Eve!

They knew the sheep was nearly awake and the magic-night-sleep over. Instead of hiding or being back in the North Pole where they normally are when the magic powder wears off, they stood over Susan, watching and waiting.

"*So you're here to help? You don't look like much help. You couldn't even avoid the magic dust,*" the cheeky elf said as Susan opened her eyes.

The other elf - the one with the round friendly face;

the one who hadn't been driving the sled when they crashed unto the hill;

the one who said they needed to slow down and get home;

the one who insisted that whizzing round the bridges was a bad idea –

he said, "*Good morning sheep! We're...*" He paused, "*Eh, sorry...you know...for the magic dust. I hope it was a nice dream?*"

Susan wasn't sure if she was awake or still dreaming. All night she had heard nothing but Christmas carols and Christmas songs. There were elves, Santa Claus, Christmas trees and presents everywhere.

You see, Santa Claus had learned another trick long ago. If people had seen you and you were going to put them to sleep, it was better to give them a Christmas dream. It meant when they woke up they never knew if what they had seen was real or part of the dream!

Susan replied, "*Yes, I am here to help, and good morning, good morning everyone. The dreams were pleasant. And I see most of the snow has melted!*"

"*That was just part of the dream,*"
snapped the cheeky elf, the one who
had crashed the sled.

The sled was in an extremely bad state.
The new power unit was broken...well
definitely not working. It was a peculiar
machine. Somehow it changed the air
in front of the sled into a frictionless
void while making the air behind the
sled expand rapidly. This combination
pushed it forward really, really quickly!
The sled runners that contained the
brakes and suspension system were
smashed to pieces. The body of the
sled had only survived because the
ground was so wet, boggy and soft.

Though they didn't realise, their
navigational system had fallen off over
the sea near Iceland. The masking tape
had become unstuck when the motor
was turned to full speed - something

they were told by the chief engineer at the EED *never* to do!

Not only was the navigational system supposed to show them their location, it also told ground control stationed at the North Pole where the sled supposedly was located. It had activated the automatic emergency rescue beacon when it fell from the sled near Iceland.

At the North Pole the emergency lights flashed red and the fateful words appeared on the screen:

 "SLED DOWN".

Search teams had rushed to the scene but could find nothing! The EED and Santa - in fact everybody at the North Pole - were extremely worried.

The reindeer instinctively knew directions so they would be able to fly home if they could get the broken sled into the air. They needed all nine reindeer though, and that was assuming the broken sled wouldn't fall apart once airborne.

While the two elves and six reindeer were stranded in the forest above Iskaheen in County Donegal, far away from the rescue operation (the biggest rescue operation ever conducted by the EED), the mood at the North Pole was grim. So grim in fact that toy production had stopped, and Santa, out of respect for the elves and reindeer had decided to stay at home this year. Shedding a tear he lamented, "*Why did we not just use the auld reindeers like every other year?!*"

In the forest the elves had enacted their emergency protocol - hide the sled, hide yourself and wait for help. But they hadn't realised that the navigational system was lost and therefore their plan was worthless!

At Susan's instruction the sled was uncovered and ropes tied to it. The six reindeer, two elves and one sheep pulled with all their might but the sled was stuck fast.

They tried again, and then again.

It didn't budge an inch!

A brilliant idea came to Susan's mind. *"I can get help! I'm friends with some highland cattle who live only a few fields away. If one of you elves could help by opening and closing gates, I'm sure they would come and lend us a hoof."*

The elves were unhappy about this plan but after a 'secret' and at times loud discussion, and only because it was Christmas Eve, they eventually agreed.

You must remember that Christmas Day starts at different times in different places. It would be Christmas Day much sooner in Christ Church (New Zealand) than Culmore (just down the road) so they needed to get on with things.

Christmas Eve, Early Morning

The elf with the round friendly face
went along with Susan. He was
amazingly nimble on his feet. He never
stood on a twig and never made a
sound when opening or closing gates.
Even when he jumped over a hedge he
landed without a sound. He was so
quiet that once in a panic Susan
thought she'd lost him, but there he
was, right beside her. She now realised
why elves are never caught!

The highland cattle were sleeping in a
circle in the middle of the field. They
were fierce looking animals with long
horns, shaggy ginger hair and a floppy
fringe that went over their eyes but
they were friendly when you got to
know them. One of the cattle,
awakened out of sleep whispered,

"*Who's that?*" (To a human it would have sounded like a low mooing sound.)

Susan whispered back, "*It's me, you know, Susan the sheep.*" "*Oh yes, Susan. I thought it was you but then wondered why on earth you would be here at this time of the morning.*" Without the usual pleasantries, Susan implored, "*I need a favour, an urgent one*".

By now all the cattle were awake, as was Dancer who was still hiding in the middle of the herd.

Susan took a deep breath and continued: "*What I need help with is going to seem too far fetched to be true, but it is true. I promise you that it's true*". "*Go on Susan,*" the highland cow replied. She took another deep breath and blurted out, "*There's a sled stuck in the forest, and it's...Santa's sled. It crashed the other night. Would some of you come and help Santa's reindeer pull it out?"*

Two things happened at once before the highland cow could reply. Firstly, Dancer having heard this, stood up in the middle of the ring of cattle and danced about (remember her name). At the same time the elf with the round normally friendly face ran into the field looking cross. He shouted at Dancer, *"Why did you run off - leaving us to it?"* Everyone was surprised, particularly Dancer who had assumed the elves had left and wouldn't be back until after Christmas! She lifted her nose into the air and replied, *"If you hadn't crashed the sled I wouldn't have needed to run for my life!"*

The elf's face was glowing red with anger. He didn't know how to do the *'Turtle from Twiggle'* who tells children and angry elves to take a breath and talk about the problem that is making you feel cross or unhappy. Instead he snapped back, "*If you and the rest of you lot (well apart from Rudolph) hadn't kept encouraging the other elf to go quicker and quicker, he might have listened to me and slowed down!*"

Before either could speak again Susan interjected, "*As I was saying, would a few of you come and help pull the sled from the trees unto the lane. It's nearly Christmas Eve and we haven't much time to spare*".

So with the argument averted and assistance secured, four of the biggest highland cattle went along to help.

The Wise Old Owl arrived just as the sled had been hauled unto the lane.

Elves don't like owls. It's not that they have anything against them personally. It's just that owls are so quiet that even elves, with all their natural awareness and training, rarely hear owls until it's too late! Sometimes on Christmas Eve, adolescent owls will buzz Santa's sled. The elves hate it because it scares them but Santa and the owls think it's funny!

The Wise Old Owl spoke: "*Good morning elves, reindeer and cattle. The sled must be taken back to the school*".

"*The sled doesn't work!*" snapped the cheeky elf.

"*Yes it is broken. However the seven reindeer will be able to get it into the air,*" replied the Wise Old Owl.

Rudely, the cheeky elf who had crashed the sled interrupted, "*No they won't*".

Head teacher Wise Owl, giving the cheeky elf a stare that even Paddington Bear would be proud of, continued without raising her voice, "*I have been told on good authority that seven reindeer will be able to pull the sled now that it's out on the lane*"

On hearing this, the reindeer without being told went to the front of the sled and formed up. The four highland cattle offered to help and this was gratefully accepted. "*Thank you for being so good,*" the Wise Old Owl said, "*For this journey the four highland cattle will go to the front, three of you reindeer will go to the back and two to each side.*"

They decided to travel over land as much as possible and only venture unto

the road when really needed. Of course
this would include near the school
where lots of people lived so they would
have to be extra careful. One elf would
go in front of the sled and the other
behind it. Susan would travel on the
sled and steer.

The Wise Old Owl left the elf with the
round friendly face in charge and flew
straight back to the school.

Above the forest and behind the sled
what looked like a shooting star
whizzed through the air but no one saw
it.

The party made their way down the
lane past the heaps of junk the false
Santa Claus had dumped. They crossed
over the road briefly to get unto the
fields that sloped down to the Foyle.

This was a remarkable journey for the cattle. When they came to a hedge or sheuch (that's a little stream) the reindeer jumped over it, taking the sled and surprised cattle with them. Every time, the cattle braced themselves for a rough landing but every time they floated to the ground gently!

Before they knew it the party had arrived back at school. Thankfully, and probably due to the early hour plus the holiday period, they had achieved the journey without being spotted by any humans.

They pressed the buzzer and were let in. The Wise Old Owl directed them into the main hall where the first thing the cattle saw was some succulent hay and gloriously fresh water.

The first thing the elves noticed was a very stern looking chief engineer from the EED with a team of rather cross-looking technicians!

Christmas Eve, Just Before Breakfast

I haven't forgotten about Prancer who had safely reached Portrush just as Boaty McBoatface was leaving. With great stealth and a little bit of flying, he sneaked unto the boat. After some searching he found a lovely (empty) cabin so decided to remain there for the rest of the journey. He closed and locked the door, then settled down for a good sleep.

The journey was completely uneventful - that's why we told you nothing about it!

That is, until they got near Iceland.

Here, and whilst in the middle of an enjoyable dream about playing in the snow, Prancer's antlers tingled so much they woke him up. Looking out the window he was able to see the EED search party.

Humans couldn't see them. All the humans saw were some strange nocturnal lights that they assumed to be the Aurora Borealis (the Northern Lights) and some odd flying object that no one could identify.

Prancer trotted straight to the deck and after a short run and jump he leaped into the sky and off to meet the EED search party. This all happened at the perfect moment because the EED (who had found the emergency beacon straightaway and were wondering why there was masking tape stuck to it) had just received word to return to the North Pole as a strange phone call had been received about the sled's actual location.

The EED team reckoned that the sled could be repaired in the main workshop but not in the school. The propulsion system wasn't working and they had been warned that under no circumstances was it to be dismantled as they had no idea how it removed gravity or created thrust. In fact they thought tampering with it may actually be catastrophically dangerous.

The chief engineer asked the Wise Old Owl if he could use the telephone in her office. After a short conversation with someone he came back and gave instructions that it was safe for the sled to be totally dismantled as it couldn't be fixed in time to use this year.

The four friends looked sad, but said nothing. The elves got to work and in a short time the sled was sitting in neat piles ready to be boxed up and carted away.

Meanwhile, on the country lane - though he never normally did it during the day - the false Santa Claus had just dumped his fifth load of junk. He was having a brilliant Christmas, the best ever!

The mood at the school was sombre. Everyone felt sad. The elf who had crashed the sled was feeling especially gloomy and even just slightly guilty.

A big red post van drove into the car park at the side of the school. It wasn't so much a van as a lorry, a rather big lorry. It drove in through the school gates and up to the top playground before reversing back to the main door.

The buzzer sounded.

Wise Old Owl and Rudolph (who had come back to the school to help after leaving Susan on Iskaheen hill) went to the door. The Wise Old Owl came back in looking stunned and amazed, and stammered to the chief engineer:

"He...he...wants to...to speak...to you."

Shortly after the engineer returned and ordered, *"Okay team, out to the lorry and bring in the boxes for this sled. There are also green and red crates. Red to the bottom of the hall, green to the top. Let's get to work".*

Then looking at the elf who had crashed the sled he said, *"Oh yes, he wants to speak to you in the office!"*

As the elf walked out, the chief engineer said under his breath, *"Bye bye, golden time".*

The cheeky elf who was now much less cheeky, didn't think this remark at all funny.

With the broken sled packed away and the new crates brought in, the elves got to work and soon two much smaller sleds sat in the main hall.

Then *he* came in. This was no false Santa!

The four children, the Wise Old Owl and the four highland cattle couldn't believe who they were looking at:

The Real Santa Claus!

"*Thank you children!*

Thank you Wise Old Owl!

Thank you highland cattle!" his great voice boomed.

"*Highland cattle, I have a very special favour to ask from you. Would you pull one of these sleds tonight?*"

The cattle stood, wide eyed and speechless. Eventually one replied, "*We would love to, but we can't fly.*"

"*So if we can fix that with a little magic dust, would you?*" Santa asked.

The four cattle nodded their heads still mesmerised by his request.

"*Now children, I need to speak to you on your own with the Wise Old Owl.*" (Remember you must never go off with a stranger on your own without an adult you know being with you.)

I won't tell you what anyone asked Santa for - well apart from Susan because she asked for something special - she asked for all the rubbish to be removed from the lane!

Just as Santa finished speaking with the children the buzzer went again and Prancer appeared. Santa looked at his watch and called, "*It's time!*"

The reindeer were tethered to one sled and the highland cattle to the other. Santa reached into his pocket and took out a little sack of magic dust and blew it round the cattle.

The two sleds were carried from the school hall to the playground. It was decided that the elf with the round friendly face would fly one sled and Santa would man the other.

The elf who had crashed the big sled was left to clear up the cow poop in the school! They'd pick him up later when they were delivering the presents in Culmore.

Before Santa left he reached into his pocket and brought out some more (slow-acting) magic dust. He blew it round the Wise Old Owl, Susan the sheep, Ralph the buzzard, Finbar the Mouse, and Betty the collie dog.

They all got home and into bed just before drifting into a deep sleep filled with wonderful Christmas scenes!

The children rose happily the next morning to find their stockings full of all the gifts they had requested.

However, when the false Santa woke up, he could not get down the stairs in his house because they were piled high with all the rubbish he had dumped at Iskaheen hill.

As there was so much of it and because it was Christmas, it cost him all the money he had made to get it disposed of properly!

The End

Printed in Great Britain
by Amazon